This book is dedicated to my best friend, Laura, ...
is an amazing role model by being ...
caring people towards all creatures, ...

Written and illustrated by Karen Plane

Trademarked under Little Fawn Creations

A little bee left its hive,
for an adventure to feel alive.
There is so much to see,
when a little bee can be free.

This little bee is full of fuzz,
flying up and down with a buzz.
Its wings are so small and sweet,
with cute, sticky and dangling feet.

This little bee was flying around
and decided to head towards the ground.
There it found a blanket with some food,
suddenly the bee was in an excited mood.

The little bee landed in a jar,
finally the sweet smell was
not so far.

Its long tongue
became sticky and
red
and eventually it
was happy and fed.

A jar filled with strawberry jam so sweet,

this made the little bee think 'what a treat.'

The little bee flew out of the jar,

suddenly, it saw a hand from afar.

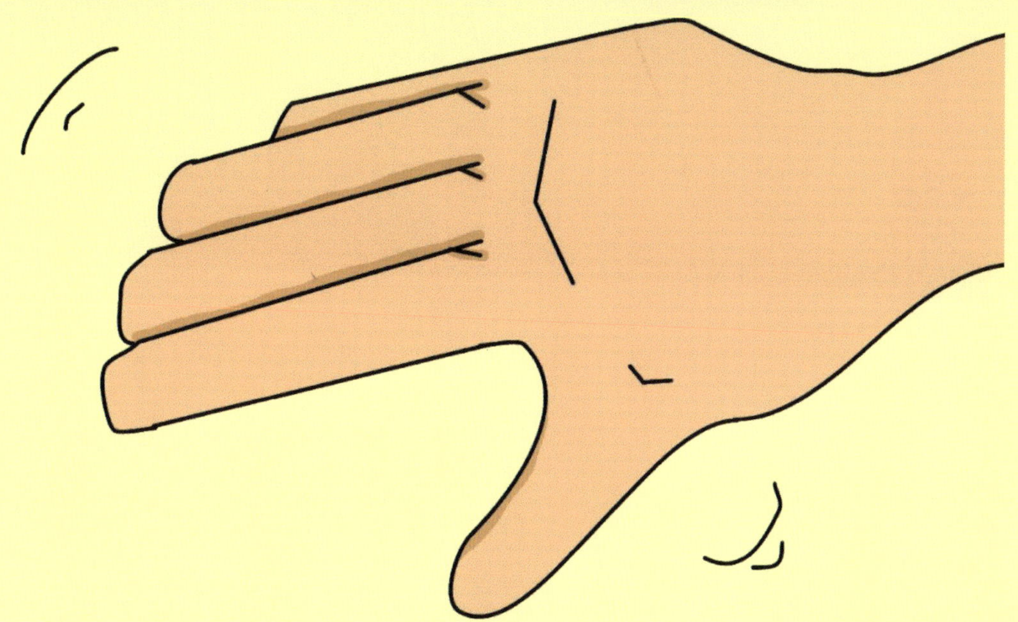

The hand swiped at the little bee,

sadly, the bee didn't understand you see.

The little bee only wanted something to taste,

not knowing the hand was moving with haste.

The little bee did not want to sting,
as it laid on the grass with a sore wing.
Had it used its stinger, it could be painful,
and the little bee would die, so we need to be careful.

The little bee needed something sweet,
suddenly it saw a pair of big feet.
A large spoon with sugar water appears,
the little bee loses all its fears.

The sugar water tasted
so good,
suddenly, its energy lifted
its mood.
The little bee's wings
started to sweep,
it lifted off wanting to
leap.

The little bee flew high in the sky,
it suddenly felt great, which was not a lie.
The little bee made a loud buzz,
as the breeze blew through its cover of fuzz.

The little bee saw a pretty flower,

and flew towards it with all of its power.

The little bee landed on a petal,

it thought, this is where I'll settle.

The little bee's tongue
started to drink,

is it sugar water, what do
you think?

No, it's sweet nectar
for this bee,

nectar helps bees make
honey; you see.

This little bee's tiny and
sticky feet,
collecting pollen in the
midday heat.

Pollen looks much like fairy
dust,
as it spreads all over with
a mighty gust.

As the little bee flies away,
the pollen on its feet began to sway.
The little bee travels far and wide,
taking the pollen on a ride.

The pollen arrives on
another flower,
it is so small but has
so much power.
In time, new blossoms
will grow,
this will help our world
you know.

The little bee flies
back to the hive,
it certainly felt lucky
to be alive.

The little bee uses the nectar
to make honey,
it is our little chef, now isn't
that funny.

Now, when you see a bee,

just leave it to be free.

We need them to keep our world alive,

so that we can all be happy and thrive.

Did You Know?

- There are over 16,000 different types of bees in the world. The most common to us are the bumble bees.
- Bees have an amazing sense of smell. They can tell the difference between the types of flowers by their receptors in their antennae.
- Bees have 5 eyes! They have an eye each on the left and right side of their heads and 3 on top.
- We use sat nav to guide us, but bees use the sun to help them with their directions.
- Bees are important! They provide 1/3 of our food supply, help make medicines, stops soil erosion, and give food to wildlife.
- The most important fact about our bees is that they support our plants that help us to breathe. Our little superheroes!

Wordsearch Puzzle

A	F	U	Z	Z	Y	Y	N	P	N
E	P	L	A	N	T	S	E	C	E
Q	U	E	E	N	R	P	C	A	N
P	S	A	H	E	F	O	T	S	P
F	Z	F	W	O	T	L	A	M	E
N	X	O	C	B	N	L	R	A	T
G	L	E	C	U	T	E	L	L	A
F	S	R	P	Z	I	N	Y	L	L
H	I	V	E	Z	M	A	F	L	S
I	W	I	N	G	S	P	F	B	L

BUZZ CUTE FLOWERS FUZZY HIVE HONEY LEAF NECTAR

PETALS PLANTS POLLEN QUEEN SMALL WINGS

Crossword Puzzle

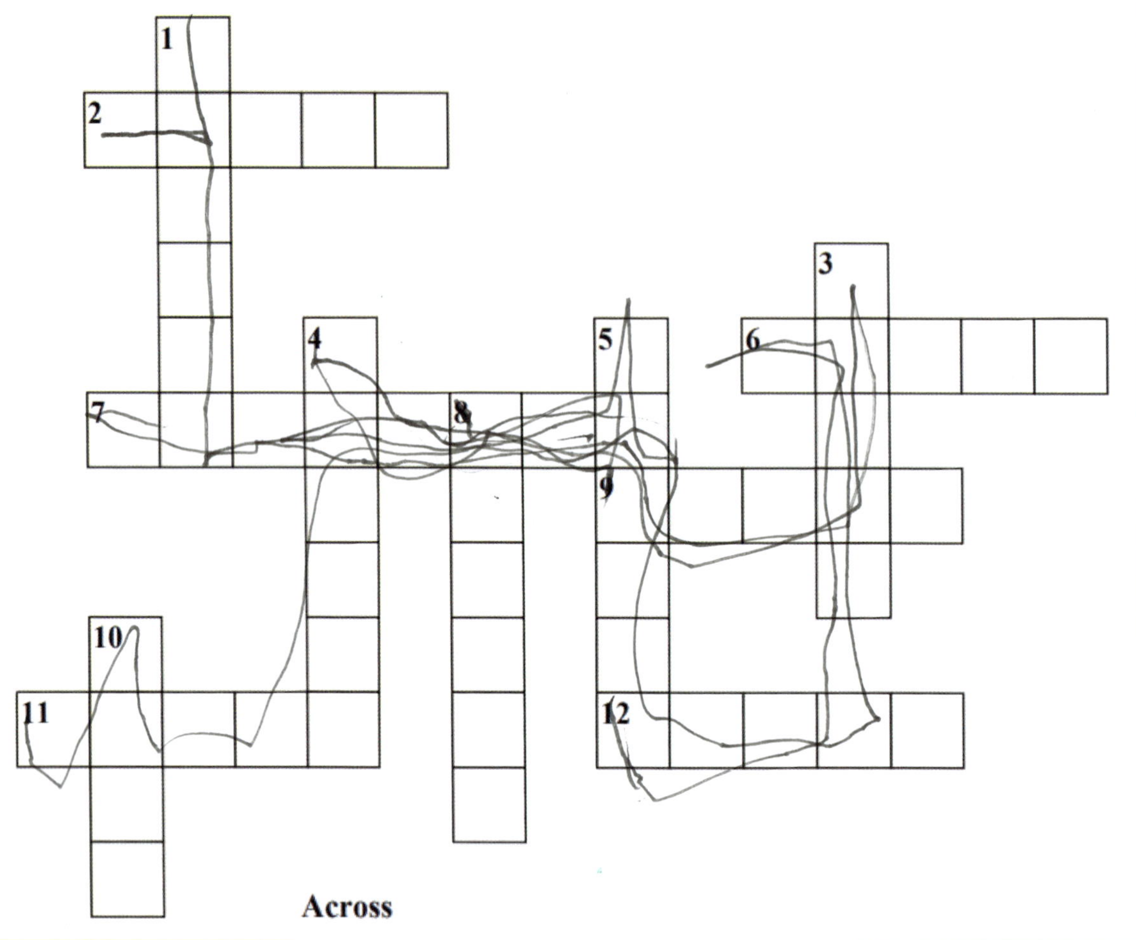

Across

[2] What do bees make that we eat?

[6] Some bees are hairy and ...

[7] Bees have a pair of receptors called ...

[9] What are big and have leaves?

[11] What helps bees fly?

[12] What is a group of bees called?

Down

[1] What do bees collect on their feet from flowers?

[3] Who is the boss of bees?

[4] What are green and seen on most plants?

[5] What are parts of a flower?

[8] What ingredient is in honey that comes from flowers?

[10] Where do some bees live?

Colour the bee and draw some flowers for it

How to save a bee recipe

Sugar water

If you see a bee laying on the ground struggling, you can feed it some sugar water to save it.

Ingredients

Teaspoon of white sugar
100ml of cold water

Method

Add the sugar to the water in a small bowl. You can keep it in a bottle if you are out and about.

Dip a teaspoon into the sugar water and carefully lay it in front of the bee. The bee's cute little tongue will start to lick the water and give it some energy to fly off.

Crossword Puzzle Answers

Down

(1) pollen
(3) queen
(4) leaves
(5) petals
(8) nectar
(10) hive

Across

(2) honey
(6) fuzzy
(7) antennae
(9) trees
(11) wings
(12) swarm

Printed in Great Britain
by Amazon

20313008R10016